Cany OFF-ROAD VEHICLE TRAILS

Canyon Rims & Needles Areas

BY

F.A. Barnes

An illustrated guide to the
backcountry roads and off-road
vehicle trails in two areas of
southeastern Utah's canyon country

1990
Canyon Country Publications

This book is the EIGHTH in a series
of practical guides to travel and recreation
in the scenic Colorado Plateau region of the
Four Corners States

All written material, maps and
photographs in this book are by F. A. Barnes
unless otherwise credited

PRINTING HISTORY
First published in 1978
by Wasatch Publishers, Salt Lake City
Reprinted in 1987
by Canyon Country Publications
Completely updated and reprinted in 1990
by Canyon Country Publications
in larger format with additional illustrations

Artwork by Kathy Nunley and F. A. Barnes

Copyright 1990
Canyon Country Publications
P. O. Box 963
Moab, UT 84532

ISBN 0-9614586-7-4
LCN 89-92058

CONTENTS

INTRODUCTION

GUIDEBOOK SERIES

This is one of a series of practical guidebooks, each one listing and describing the off-road vehicle trails within one or more distinct areas of the canyon country of southeastern Utah. Each of these areas is defined by a combination of man-made boundaries, such as highways, and natural barriers that bar travel by off-road vehicle, such as rivers.

AREAS COVERED BY THIS BOOK

This book covers two distinct areas. One area, which lies to the south and west of Moab, is called the "Canyon Rims Area" for the purposes of this book. It is defined by U.S. 191 on the east, the Colorado River on the west and Utah 211 and lower Indian Creek Canyon on the south. This area includes all of the Bureau of Land Management's "Canyon Rims Recreation Area."

The second area is still farther south of Moab and is called the "Needles Area" for the purposes of this book. It is defined by Utah 211 and lower Indian Creek Canyon on the north, the Colorado River on the west, the northeastern boundary of the Dark Canyon Primitive Area and the Abajo Mountains on the south, and U.S. 191 on the east. This area includes all of the Needles District of Canyonlands National Park.

The map on the inside-front cover of this book shows the boundaries of the two areas covered.

SUPPLEMENTARY INFORMATION

Other guidebooks in the *Canyon Country* series contain supplementary information concerning perimeter and access roads, natural history, hiking, camping, archeology, other modes of exploration, facilities, supplies and services, and the parks in these areas. See **Further Reading** in the back of this book.

AREA TERRAIN

The Canyon Rims Area contains three general types of terrain. One lies between Moab Valley and Cane Creek Canyon. This area is extremely distorted, eroded and spectacular, with deep canyons, great masses of slickrock domes and fins and a few relatively level sandflats. This area is known locally as "Behind the Rocks" because it is "behind" the southwestern rock wall of Moab Valley.

The second distinct type of terrain within the Canyon Rims Area occupies the eastern and central section of the area, and is essentially high, rolling sage-plains studded with scattered outcroppings of colorful slickrock and cut by a complex of shallow washes and canyons. This desert is terminated on the south, west and northeast by a series of deep, sheer-walled canyons.

The third type of terrain in this area lies between these cliffs and the rim of the Colorado River gorge. Most of this area is strangely eroded, dark red sandstone and sediments and red-sand desert broken by colorful rock outcroppings. The area is cut by a series of deep, labyrinthine canyons that ultimately join the Colorado River gorge.

Most of the Needles Area is a vast expanse of colorful, ancient sandstone that has been eroded into a maze-like complex of canyons, spires, domes, fins, ridges, arches, caves and other beautiful and unusual landforms. As this unique area blends into the Abajo Mountain foothills, the canyon-slashed highlands there are a second type of terrain within the Needles Area. The entire Needles Area is known for its many spectacular natural arches, its park-like meadows surrounded by walls of color-banded spires, or "needles," and its hundreds of fascinating archeological sites. The extreme eastern end of the Needles Area, in the vicinity of U.S. 191, is relatively open, rolling desert studded with eroded sandstone outcroppings.

MAPS

Commercial. Wasatch Publishers issues a large map titled *Canyon Country* OFF-ROAD VEHICLE TRAIL MAP - **Canyon Rims & Needles Areas** that shows the approximate alignment of the trails described in this book. This map is available from various retail outlets throughout canyon country. The map is based upon the U.S.G.S. 1:62,500 scale topographic quadrangles that cover the Canyon Rims and Needles areas, but with information added to make them more useful. Parts of the areas covered by this book appear on a 1:62,500 scale commercial geologic map of Canyonlands National Park. This map is excellent for its purpose, but has little value for exploring backcountry roads and trails. Another commercial map, titled *Canyon Country's* **CANYON RIMS RECREATION AREA MAP,** gives more details about that section of the Canyon Rims area.

U.S. Geological Survey. The areas covered by this guidebook are shown on several different sets of U.S.G.S. maps. In addition to the 1:62,500 scale 15 minute series, they are depicted on a 1:250,000 scale topographic quadrangle of the United States Series titled Moab and on two 1:100,000 scale metric-series quadrangles titled Moab and La Sal. These maps show the general region, but are of very limited value during actual explorations. The U.S.G.S. 1:62,500 scale topographic quadrangles are not up to date on backcountry roads and off-road vehicle trails.

There is also a 1:24,000 series of U.S.G.S. quadrangles. These maps are largely up to date with respect to roads and trails but, due to their scale, too many are required for general backcountry exploration. Many of the trails described in this book are shown on the U.S.G.S. metric series maps, but some trails shown are either incomplete or inaccurate, and the maps do not provide adequate guidance to the terrain.

Parts of the areas covered by this book also appear on a U.S.G.S. 1:62,500 scale topographic map of Canyonlands National Park. These and the other U.S.G.S. maps can be obtained through any U.S.G.S. retail or mail outlet. Some can be purchased from various visitor centers and retail outlets within canyon country.

Utah State. The Utah Department of Transportation issues an official highway map that is useful for access routes to canyon country, but shows very few backcountry roads and off-road vehicle trails. The Utah Travel Council issues a series of multipurpose regional maps of the state. Of this series, the one titled "Southeastern Utah" shows the areas covered by this book, but is of very limited value for off-highway explorations.

National Park Service. The National Park Service issues small maps of each of the districts of Canyonlands National Park, but these lack enough detail for practical backcountry use.

NAVIGATION

Navigation of canyon country off-road vehicle trails is seldom simple. Several factors combine to make maps and map-reading skills essential, and even then easy trail-finding is not always assured. Some of the factors that complicate navigation are natural, but the worst are human in origin.

The principal natural factors are terrain that lacks features prominent enough to appear on topographic maps, and stretches of sand and slickrock that show few permanent traces of the trails that penetrate them.

Of the human factors, one is the lack of directional and name signs. A few of the trail and road junctions in the area covered by this book are marked by signs, but most are not.

The greatest single problem to navigation, however, is mineral search activity that obscures or realigns established trails, creates new trails, or laces huge areas with parallel and intersecting trails in support of seismographic surveys. Such operations can, within a few days, turn a huge unspoiled natural area that was penetrated by a single obscure trail or none, into a veritable maze of bulldozed, eroding trails that destroy the natural beauty and either end at a drill site or go nowhere at all.

Since existing laws governing the search for and extraction of minerals from public land do not prevent such abusive activities, those who intend to explore canyon country by off-road vehicle must be prepared for the resulting navigational problems. The trails described in this book have all been traveled personally by its author, but as long as the mineral industry has the right to change existing trails and create new ones, there can be no assurance that any trail description will remain valid indefinitely.

Because of the noted natural and human factors, optimum trail navigation in much of canyon country consists of the skillful use of maps and the verbal descriptions in this book, plus trail-reading abilities, persistence and, in some cases, an element of luck. Only a few of the trails described are so well defined, and so protected by the surrounding terrain, that they can be followed without the use of navigational skills.

BASE CAMPS

The Canyon Rims and Needles areas can be explored from a variety of base camps. There are motels and commercial campgrounds in and near Moab and Monticello, and a commercial campground near the entrance to the Needles District of Canyonlands National Park. There are developed public campgrounds within Canyonlands National Park, Canyon Rims Recreation Area and Newspaper Rock State Park. Except within the national park, near developed areas, and on a few posted parcels of private land, primitive camping is permitted anywhere within the areas covered by this book. It should be noted that there are virtually no other traveler amenities in the vicinity of these two areas except at the nearby communities of Moab and Monticello, Utah. Automotive fuel and limited camping supplies are usually available at the commercial campground near the park entrance.

Primitive camping, upper Lavender Canyon

SEASONS

Because of the high-desert climate that prevails throughout the non-mountainous areas of canyon country, the best seasons for exploring the Canyon Rims and Needles areas are spring, March through May, and fall, September through November. Exploration is possible during the summer, however, although daytime temperatures are generally in the 90s. Most of these areas can also be explored during normal winters, although even light snow may make the steeper stretches of some trails impassable.

The trails that enter the Abajo Mountain foothill highlands are generally closed by snow during the winter, except to those equipped with snowshoes, cross-country skis or snowmobiles, but are normally open from April through November. Off-road vehicle explorers planning trips on these higher trails in the spring or late fall should first check trail conditions at the U.S. Forest Service office in Monticello.

ACCESS ROADS - CANYON RIMS AREA

General. Access to the Canyon Rims Area from its perimeter highways, U.S. 191 and Utah 211, is by way of one road that is partly paved and partly graveled, and another paved road that has a gravel road spur. For the purposes of this book, all access roads have been given names by the author, if they do not already have them, names that are based upon nearby natural or man-made features. All of these interior access roads are shown on one or both of the commercial maps noted earlier. The gravel roads are usually passable to two-wheel drive vehicles, but may have local bad spots or may be in generally bad condition due to recent precipitation, heavy mineral exploration traffic, lack of maintenance, or some combination of these factors.

Cane Creek Road. This paved road leaves U.S. 191 (Main Street) five blocks south of the center of Moab (Center Street), provides access to a major subdivision, then parallels the cliffs to the southwest of Moab before entering the Colorado River gorge. There, it travels downriver between the river and cliffs for about 3 miles before entering lower Cane Creek Canyon. The pavement ends just before the road enters the canyon. The road is graveled from there on to where it ends, about 7 miles up Cane Creek Canyon. For the purposes of this book, Cane Creek Road is considered to end where it reaches a ford of Cane Creek, because this crossing is often not passable to two-wheel drive vehicles. As the road continues beyond the Cane Creek ford, it is called the Hurrah Pass trail in this book.

Needles Overlook Road. This paved road leaves U.S. 191 about 33 miles south of Moab, and about 12 miles south of La Sal Junction. The road penetrates the Canyon Rims Recreation Area, passes Wind Whistle Campground, then ends at the Needles Overlook, an outstanding plateau-rim viewpoint.

Anticline Overlook Road. This good graveled road spurs north from the Needles Overlook Road about 16 miles from U.S. 191. It travels the high mesa-top of Hatch Point. About 9 miles from the road's junction with the Needles Overlook Road, a short spur road to the east goes to Hatch Point Campground. The main road continues north to end at the point's northernmost extremity, Anticline Overlook, which offers a spectacular view down into the lower canyon country that surrounds this lofty vantage point. A short spur road to the west beyond the campground junction goes to a spectacular and colorful view of the Colorado River gorge.

11

Others. There are several backcountry graded-dirt roads within the Canyon Rims Recreation Area that are normally passable to most highway vehicles. These are described in a book titled *Canyon Country's* **CANYON RIMS RECREATION AREA,** and are shown on the matching map.

ACCESS ROADS - NEEDLES AREA

All access into the Needles Area is from its main access road, Utah 211, or from U.S. Forest Service roads that approach the area from the Abajo Mountains to the south. All off-road vehicle trails described in this area begin from Utah 211 or its extension into Canyonlands National Park, or spur from another trail.

Six Shooter Peaks, from Utah 211

TRAIL DESCRIPTION FORMAT

Trail name: For the purposes of this book, each trail segment described has been given a name. Where trail names are in popular use, or have appeared in print, these were used. For trails with no name history, names were assigned. Most of these were chosen from named geographic features near the trail, but in a few cases appropriate names were assigned by the author.

Type. As an aid to those who use this book, trail segments are classified into three types, "spur," "connecting" and "loop." A "spur" trail is a dead-end trail that has no practical connections with other trails anywhere near its end. A "connecting" trail is one that connects two or more other listed access roads or trails. A "loop" trail is one that, as described, begins and ends from the same access road or other trail, although not necessarily from the same point. A loop trail may have spurs, and may even be joined by a connecting trail, but is still a distinct stretch of trail that is worth traveling as a loop.

Maps. In this section of the trail description format, the maps most useful in navigating the trail are listed. The U.S.G.S. 1:62,500 scale topographic quadrants that cover the Canyon Rims and Needles areas are not listed because their backcountry trail information is generally not up to date, and the current U.S.G.S 7-1/2 minute maps are not listed because too many are required for practical navigation and they are not readily available.

Mileage. Approximate mileages are given for each trail segment. For spur trails, the round trip distance is given. If a spur trail has other spurs, one-way mileages for these generally appear within the trail description. For connecting trails, the one-way distance is given. For loop trails, the one-way distance is given, exclusive of any spurs along the loop. One-way mileages for such spurs may appear within the trail descriptions.

Time. Because of the wide variety of surfaces and hazards encountered on canyon country off-road vehicle trails, plus other variables such as driving and navigational skills and time spent at stops along the way, the times to travel specific trails can only be approximated. The times given are based upon the author's experience, with all these variables taken into consideration. In each case, those who choose to "challenge the trail" will find little difficulty in bettering the times given, but in doing so will have missed most of the value of that trail.

Difficulty. Trail segments are given general ratings as to their difficulty, not for the purpose of a challenge, but to help drivers with limited experience select trails within their capabilities. Three ratings are used: "easy," "moderate" and "difficult." Such ratings are always subject to debate, because they involve personal judgment, and because no one trail is uniform for its entire length. A trail may be quite rough or difficult for most of its length, yet have easy stretches. Conversely, a trail may be predominantly two-wheel drive, yet have short stretches that are difficult even for four-wheel drive. Thus, the difficulty ratings given should be taken only in the most general sense, with exceptions to be expected along the way. In addition to trail ratings, trail surface conditions are listed under this heading. A trail may be very rough, even though rated "easy." Where there are unusually difficult or hazardous places along a trail, these are noted in the trail description.

Access. There is generally more than one access route to each trail segment, and the one chosen will depend upon the direction of approach. In some cases, one suggested access route is given. Those who prefer to use another route can do so by using the appropriate map, although some trails are easier to find and navigate in one direction than the other.

Trail summary. In this section, a brief summary is given of the trail's scenic highlights and other points of interest, as an aid to the selection of trails to explore.

Trail description. Each trail segment is described here at greater length than in the summary. The descriptions cover access details, trail conditions, scenic and other highlights, spur trails where these exist, and other points of interest. In no case are such descriptions complete. Many details and highlights are left for explorers to discover for themselves, but enough are given to help those with limited time to select suitable trails, and to provide a few points to watch for along the way. With loop trails, the description will begin at the loop-end that is recommended as a starting point. Explorers should consider all mileages noted in this section as approximate, since odometer accuracy varies from vehicle to vehicle.

Notes. Miscellaneous information related to each trail is listed in this final section of the trail description format.

AREA NOTES

1. The paved highways that border the Canyon Rims and Needles areas are not described in this book, but are covered in other volumes of the Canyon Country guidebook series. Both of these highways are highly scenic.

2. The trails in the Canyon Rims and Needles areas are described as "trail segments" because some of them are interconnected, making it impractical to define them otherwise. These trail segments can be explored individually, or by linking two or more together into routes that take half a day or more to travel. A few such routes are suggested in one section of this book.

3. Many of the trail segments listed have stretches that can be traveled by two-wheel drive, but all require off-road vehicles if their entire lengths are to be explored.

4. Those exploring the off-road vehicle trails in the Canyon Rims and Needles areas, especially single vehicles, are advised to travel prepared for problems such as mechanical failure or getting stuck. Items that should always be carried are a spare tire, extra fuel, tools and plenty of water. An additional safety margin is afforded vehicles equipped with winches, heavy-duty roll bars and extra food in the form of freeze-dried meals.

5. Although CB radios may be of some value in calling for assistance, this value is limited during the daylight hours because of poor line-of-sight characteristics in much of the canyon country region. Night transmissions will reach farther because of atmospheric "bounce effects."

6. All historic and prehistoric sites and artifacts on public land are protected by a variety of state and federal laws. Such artifacts should not be collected, and sites should be left undisturbed.

7. Occasionally, old mines are reactivated. In order to avoid possible injury and conflict, such mines, and all equipment and activities associated with them, should be avoided.

8. Individual trail descriptions sometimes note that a trail junction "may" be marked by a sign. There are two reasons why the author could not be positive about such signs. One: vandals sometimes remove, destroy or "collect" such signs, even though such activities violate either federal or state laws. Two: of the various federal and state land administration agencies involved, only the National Park Service has an active and effective program for marking vehicle trail junctions with directional signs, then maintaining them. Thus, when one of the few non-Park Service signs is vandalized, it may or may not be replaced.

9. Some of the trails within the Abajo foothills area are at elevations that receive snow in late fall or early winter, and this snow generally lasts until late spring. This leaves a short season for exploring these higher trails.

10. There are many interconnecting off-road vehicle trail segments within the Canyon Rims Recreation Area that are not described in this guidebook. Most of these are worth exploring if time permits. These trails are described and shown in the book and matching map about this large BLM recreation area.

11. During the warmer months, potable water is available at the two developed campgrounds in the Canyon Rims Recreation Area. All natural water sources in that area have been heavily contaminated by grazing livestock.

12. Most of the trails described within the Needles Area are in, or partly in, Canyonlands National Park. Park regulations require that vehicles operated on such trails be highway-licensed for the state in which the owner lives, that vehicle operators bear valid drivers licenses, and that all vehicles stay strictly on the designated roads and trails. These regulations are enforced.

13. Those using this book will find that some of the trails described show very few signs of current usage. That is because such trails get very little recreational use and only sporadic mineral-search use. Despite this, the author has explored each of the trails listed and found it to be worth sharing with those who are interested in the canyon country hinterlands.

14. Most of the trails in the Canyon Rims and Needles areas can be traveled by skillfully-driven sand buggies, trail-type motorcycles, mountain bikes and other wheeled vehicles with off-road capabilities.

TRAIL SEGMENTS

CANYON RIMS AREA

Moab Valley from Moab Rim

TRAIL DESCRIPTIONS

Trail Name: AMASA BACK

Map: *Canyon Country* OFF-ROAD VEHICLE TRAIL MAP - Canyon Rims & Needles Areas

Time: 4 hours; longer if the two spurs are explored

Type: Spur

Mileage: 8 miles round trip

Difficulty: moderate, but very rough in places, with the trail surface largely packed sediments, broken rock and slickrock, with some wash sand and drift sand.

Access: this trail is a spur of Cane Creek Road.

Trail Summary: the trail crosses deep Cane Creek Canyon and ascends onto an immense sandstone ridge that is isolated by the Colorado River gorge and Cane Creek Canyon, offering outstanding views at many points along its short length.

Amasa Back trail above Jackson Hole, upper left

Trail Description:

The trail spurs right from Cane Creek Road about 1-1/4 miles after that road enters the mouth of Cane Creek Canyon. The trail junction is inconspicuous. Between the road and the canyon bottom, the trail descends steep, rocky slopes. Depending upon the season, there may be flowing water in Cane Creek. The trail crosses the creek, then travels along the canyon wall on rocky terraces for the first mile or so, climbing as it goes. After almost 2 miles, the trail forks. The left spur ends in a lovely box-end canyon in about 1 mile and is worth exploring. The main trail goes right, climbs onto still higher ground, then skirts along the lofty rim of Jackson Hole, which is a "rincon," or abandoned meander of the Colorado River.

At one point near the rim a trail spurs to the right. This spur crosses some sandflats, then ends at a slickrock rim where a pipeline descends into the rivergorge. The view upriver from this rim overlook is outstanding. The main trail continues along the rim of Jackson Hole, offering panoramic views of this feature, the river beyond, the potash plant beside the river and the redrock cliffs beyond. The described trail ends near where a pipeline and several utility lines cross a narrow neck in the high Amasa Back ridgeline, although some vehicles have gone beyond this point. Exploring the immense sandstone ridge of Amasa Back by hiking is worthwhile.

Notes:

1. If the water flow in Cane Creek is heavy from recent precipitation, do not attempt to ford the creek.

2. A large and beautiful natural span called Funnel Arch is visible from various points along the first 2 miles of this trail. The arch is on a terrace above Cane Creek Road on the east side of the canyon, but is not visible from that road.

3. The stretch of this trail along the Jackson Hole rim is hazardous. Careful driving is required.

Trail Name: CANE CREEK CANYON

Map: *Canyon Country* OFF-ROAD VEHICLE TRAIL MAP - Canyon Rims & Needles Areas

Time: 6 hours; longer if the trail has been damaged by recent flooding

Type: Connecting

Mileage: 13 miles

Difficulty: moderate, but very rough in places, with the trail surface largely packed sediments, washbottom rocks and sand and creek fords, with some drift sand, mud and slickrock.

Access: this trail connects U.S. 191 with the Hurrah Pass trail and Cane Creek Road

Trail Summary: this trail travels the lovely, wooded narrows of upper Cane Creek Canyon, then the broad and spectacular central section of this long gorge, before connecting with Cane Creek Road and the Hurrah Pass trail near the narrow lower part of the canyon.

Cane Creek Canyon Trail, upper Cane Creek Canyon

Trail Description:

The trail leaves U.S. 191 just a few yards north of "Hole-'n-the-Rock," a tourist attraction about 16 miles south of Moab. The trail spurs right from the highway, then drops down into narrow, wooded upper Cane Creek Canyon. There is usually flowing water in this canyon for the first two miles or more. The trail closely parallels the stream for about 1-1/2 miles, fording it now and then. As the verdant canyon narrows still further, the trail drops more steeply, then reaches a side-canyon from the left. Here, near a small waterfall and some pools in the slickrock, the trail descends a rocky ledge and crosses the sidecanyon drainage. As the main stream descends through a series of pools and narrow clefts, the trail climbs higher to travel narrow terraces above the bottom of the gorge, then descend farther on to cross the stream. In this vicinity the trail is usually indistinct because of frequent washouts, but in general either of two routes can be taken for the next 3 or 4 miles.

One route follows the easiest path beside or near the stream course and on about the same level. This is usually the quickest route, but can offer problems with washbottom rock, bogs and sand. The other route travels the remnant of an old mining trail on a terrace of sediments to the right, above the stream bed. This route affords a better view of the surrounding canyon, because it is above most of the dense washbottom vegetation, but is sometimes difficult to follow because of erosion-gullies that have cut it, narrow places, fallen boulders and other hazards. A short distance before this route finally becomes impassable, a spur left from a broad, open stretch of terrace angles steeply down to the stream course and joins the other route.

From here on for several miles, traveling this trail becomes a matter of following the most heavily used set of wheel tracks through the canyon-bottom undergrowth and trees, and avoiding the soft sand and mudhole hazards that false trails encounter. At one point just beyond a stream course crossing near an embankment, the trail ascends a bull-dozed cut in the embankment beside a gnarled cottonwood tree. Above this cut the creek-bottom trail rejoins the old road on the higher terrace. If this inconspicuous cut is missed it is difficult, but not impossible, to rejoin the old road farther down the canyon.

The terrace road continues on down Cane Creek Canyon, crossing many badly eroded washes and skirting around giant boulders that have fallen from the cliffs above. Eventually the trail forks. The right spur travels a short distance, then ends, but is worth exploring. The main trail soon crosses the creek bottom again, then ends by connecting with the Hurrah Pass trail about 1/4 mile beyond the ford.

Notes:

1. The narrow, upper 3 miles of Cane Creek Canyon are subject to occasional flash-flooding. This realigns the trail and usually damages the ramp at the first major side-canyon. If this ramp is badly damaged, the trail is impassable until it is repaired. For this reason, it is better to travel down the canyon than up. If the ramp is impassable, it is easier to retrace 1-1/2 miles to U.S. 191 than to return the length of Cane Creek Canyon.

2. At one point in the upper canyon narrows, a picturesque old wooden bridge spans a rocky chasm.

3. The strange, stream-cut grotto below the first side-canyon can be explored by hiking back up the stream from where the trail crosses it below the grotto.

4. It is not advisable to enter upper Cane Creek Canyon if rain seems imminent in the vicinity.

Cane Creek, upper Cane Creek Canyon

Trail Name: CANE CREEK CANYON RIM

Map: *Canyon Country* OFF-ROAD VEHICLE TRAIL MAP - Canyon Rims & Needles Areas

Time: 6 hours, whether returning by the same route or leaving via Pritchett Canyon

Type: Connecting

Mileage: 15 miles one way

Difficulty: easy, with the trail largely packed or soft drift sand, broken rock, slickrock or packed sediments, with a little wash sand. Leaving via Pritchett Canyon is difficult.

Access: this trail connects U.S. 191 with the Pritchett Canyon-Behind the Rocks trail in three places.

Trail Summary: this trail crosses the open sandflats in the southeastern part of Behind the Rocks, passes a huge, colorful outcropping of slickrock that contains two interesting arches, then reaches and travels closely parallel to the high eastern rim of spectacular Cane Creek Canyon for several miles before ending at a point opposite Hurrah Pass and Anticline Overlook.

La Sal Mountains, from Cane Creek Canyon Rim trail

24

Trail Description:

The trail spurs west from U.S. 191 at the summit of the Blue Hill grade, about 13 miles south of Moab. It crosses a cattleguard, then winds through pinyon-juniper forest. About 1/2 mile from U.S. 191 the Pritchett Canyon-Behind the Rocks trail spurs right. The main trail continues toward and across the broad, open sandflats that lie between Bridger Jack Mesa and the sandstone-fin maze of Behind the Rocks. About 3-1/4 miles from the highway a spur trail to the left is worth exploring if time permits. There are several other spurs in the first 5 miles of this trail, but most are not worth exploring.

About 5-3/4 miles from the trail start it reaches a spur to the right that goes along the southern side of a huge, red sandstone ridge. This spur connects with the Pritchett Canyon-Behind the Rocks trail in the vicinity of Picture Frame Arch on the northern side of the ridge. The main Cane Creek Canyon Rim trail continues beyond this ridge offering excellent views to the east, then drops down into lower terrain. There are large quantities of chert in this area.

About 1-3/4 miles beyond the sandstone ridge the trail is joined by the Pritchett Canyon-Behind the Rocks trail coming in from the right. This trail goes right again in a few yards. About 1-1/4 miles beyond this junction in a shallow canyon, a short walk to the left of the trail goes to the breathtaking rim of a major spur of Cane Creek Canyon, just below where a shallow wash drops into a deep gorge. About 2 miles beyond this point, and just after the trail has climbed up from a lower terrace along the Cane Creek Canyon rim, a short spur trail to the left ends within a short walk of a viewpoint on the canyon rim.

For the next 4-1/4 miles the main trail parallels the lofty rim of beautiful Cane Creek Canyon, quite closely in places. Hikes to the rim anywhere along this stretch offer outstanding views of the canyon. About 1-3/4 miles beyond the first rim spur an inconspicuous trail junction is reached. The main Cane Creek Canyon Rim trail continues parallel to the rim, while the more apparent trail swings to the right and starts descending into the wild terrain to the east. This spur connects a third time with the Pritchett Canyon-Behind the Rocks trail in about 1 mile, and may be used to continue on to Pritchett Arch and on out via Pritchett Canyon.

From this junction the main trail continues on near the rim, to reach an old drill-site in about 1-3/4 miles. From this leveled area, the trail climbs a dirt embankment on the left, then continues on closely parallel to the rim.

About 1/4 mile beyond the drill site the trail travels within a few feet of the rim, offering an excellent view. Within another 1/2 mile the trail ends at the base of a small, flat-topped slickrock dome right on the rim. The view from this dome is superb in all directions. There is a mined area directly below, Cane Creek Canyon sprawls in both directions, Hurrah Pass and Anticline Overlook are on the opposite side of the canyon, a series of potash solar evaporation ponds obscure the open red desert below Dead Horse Point beyond the Colorado River, and the northern reaches of Island-in-the-Sky are visible on the western skyline.

Notes:

1. The lovely, colorful area just back from the rim beyond the trail-end viewpoint has been devastated by drilling operations in support of past uranium mining directly below the viewpoint.

2. This trail is difficult to navigate for the last mile, where it crosses stretches of slickrock and is confused by mineral search trails.

Cane Creek Canyon, from Cane Creek Canyon Rim

26

Trail Name: CHICKEN CORNERS

Map: *Canyon Country* OFF-ROAD VEHICLE TRAIL MAP - Canyon Rims & Needles Areas

Time: 4 hours; longer if the spur trail is explored, or much time is spent at the natural bridge or caves near the trail

Type: Spur

Mileage: 18 miles round trip

Difficulty: easy, with the trail largely packed drift sand and sediments, slickrock and some wash sand.

Access: this trail is one of two that continue beyond the end of the Hurrah Pass trail. It also connects with the Lockhart Basin trail about midway along its length.

Trail Summary: this trail travels the colorful, remote rimlands of the Colorado River gorge downriver from Hurrah Pass, to end at a spectacular viewpoint south of Dead Horse Point and on the opposite side of the river.

Chicken Corners, Colorado River gorge rim

Trail Description:

The trail begins at the western end of the Hurrah Pass trail, where the Jackson Hole trail descends into a narrow, rocky canyon, then heads upriver. This canyon may be fenced, but a gate allows passage. Shortly beyond this junction, the Chicken Corners trail branches. One route continues up a short canyon, then climbs out to cross a stretch of sand flats before joining the other route in about 1 mile, near the river-gorge rim.

The recommended route ascends a steep, rocky slope a few yards beyond the Jackson Hole trail junction. Within 1/2 mile this route reaches a river-bluff overlook, where a short walk out onto the slickrock rim provides a panoramic view of the river. For the next several miles the trail closely parallels the river, offering delightful views down onto its colorful gorge. About 2-1/4 miles from the trail start a fork appears. The main trail continues ahead here, but the spur trail is worth exploring, for a short distance at least. This spur skirts around the left side of a large mass of dark red sandstone that is riddled with natural caves that water erosion has created. Beyond the caves this spur trail offers two major branches. One enters a large sidecanyon and goes to several old mine sites The other climbs onto scenic benchlands at the mouth of this canyon.

The main Chicken Corners trail continues beyond this spur trail junction, parallel to the river. About 4-1/4 miles from the trail start, as it is close to the rim of a small canyon that drains into the Colorado, there is a curious natural bridge just a few feet from the trail. This bridge is inconspicuous because it is flat on top, it does not stand out from the cliff edge very far, and its top is only a little below the trail level. It formed in the fossiliferous, gray-colored limestone that rims the rivergorge and its tributaries in this area. It is worth the effort to hike down below this unusual natural bridge.

Beyond the bridge the trail continues parallel to the rivergorge but farther back from its rim. Slightly tilted geologic strata cause the trail to climb gradually, and the rivergorge to get deeper. About 5 miles from the trail start, at a point where it crosses a shallow wash near a sandstone bluff, the trail forks. This inconspicuous junction, which may be marked by a sign or rock cairn, is where the Lockhart Basin trail spurs left. The remains of an old rock wall can be seen by traveling a few yards up this wash, to where the Lockhart Basin trail climbs out of the wash on the left. Allegedly, this wall was built by horse thieves to hold stolen stock in this spring-watered canyon for later recovery and sale, although the spring is largely dry now.

Beyond this trail junction the main trail skirts along the base of various red sandstone bluffs until one forces it to the rivergorge rim. This short stretch of narrow, rim-edge trail is called "Chicken Corners." The trail continues beyond this breathtaking overlook for about 1-1/2 miles before ending at another spectacular canyon rim overlook opposite Dead Horse Point and about 450 feet above the river level.

Notes:

1. This trail is listed as a "spur," even though it connects with the Lockhart Basin trail about midway in its length, because most usage of the Chicken Corners trail will not involve that connection.

2. The short, hazardous stretch that gave this trail its name was given that name by a Moab tour guide because many of his passengers were "chicken" and preferred to walk the more dangerous few yards. This stretch of trail was once far more hazardous than it is now.

3. A wide variety of sea-life fossils can be found in the gray limestone deposit that is exposed along much of this trail.

4. Those who choose to explore the caves near this trail should take along flashlights and be alert. Rattlesnakes have been seen in these caves, even though rarely.

Trail Name: H A R T S   P O I N T

Map: *Canyon Country* OFF-ROAD VEHICLE TRAIL MAP - Canyon Rims & Needles Areas

Time: 6 hours; longer if any of the many spur trails along the way are explored

Type: Spur

Mileage: 37 miles round trip

Difficulty: easy, except for one steep, rough stretch about 1-1/2 miles from where it ends. Most of the trail is graded dirt or packed drift sand, with a little rough slickrock and rubble for the last 3 miles. Some of the many spur trails are moderate to difficult, depending on how far they are traveled.

Access: this trail is a major spur from Utah 211.

Trail Summary: this trail provides access into the high and isolated Harts Point district of Canyon Rims Recreation Area, with many scenic viewpoint near the trail and numerous spur trails, including one to remote and lovely Aqueduct Arch.

View from end of Harts Point trail

Trail Description:

The trail spurs right, or west, from Utah 211 about 6 miles from Photograph Gap, a low pass with a few old dwellings, or about 9 miles from U.S. 191. For the first 7 miles there are several spurs from the main trail. Some of these are worth exploring if time permits. About 11 miles from Utah 211 a spur trail angles right from the main trail. This spur goes generally northeastward onto a peninsula between two tributary canyons of huge and complex Harts Draw. One of these canyons contains beautiful Aqueduct Arch, an old and graceful natural span in the top of the sheer cliffs that wall the inner canyon.

Getting to this arch is one of the highlights of this trail segment. The spur trail that goes toward the arch is an old seismograph trail. About 2-1/4 miles from the main trail, turn right on a obscure spur trail that meanders through the pinyon-juniper forest in a generally southeastward direction, heading for the canyon, opposite a high, flat-topped mesa. At the end of this trail, hike on down the slickrock-and-sand terraces toward the mesa. Aqueduct Arch will soon be visible, but still far below, on the opposite side of the canyon, below the mesa and in the top of the inner-canyon slickrock wall. It is possible to hike on down to the canyon rim directly opposite the arch and on the same level, but climbing aids are needed to descend into the canyon below the span.

Aqueduct Arch

31

Beyond the Aqueduct Arch spur trail junction the main trail continues out onto Harts Point, to pass an old windmill and corral in about 3 miles. There are two more spur trails to the right beyond the windmill. About 1-1/2 miles beyond the last spur, the main trail appears to end at a narrow neck in the peninsula, but actually spurs right a few yards before the narrows. From this inconspicuous trail fork, the main trail descends steeply to a lower level, to end in another mile or so at the ultimate end of Harts Point. There are excellent views from the plateau rim at the end of the trail. The sweeping panoramic view from there includes the upper stretches of lower Indian Creek Canyon, much of Canyonlands National Park and, on clear days, the Abajo and Henry mountain ranges.

Notes:

1. There are many places along this trail where short hikes to the west lead to breathtaking views down into upper Indian Creek Canyon, the beautiful and complex canyon system traveled by Utah 211 on its way to the Needles District of Canyonlands National Park. Hikes and spur trails to the east of the main trail provide glimpses of the immense Harts Draw canyon system.

2. Golden eagles are sometimes observed in the Harts Draw canyon area.

3. For further details about the Harts Point area, refer to the book, *Canyon Country's* **CANYON RIMS RECREATION AREA,** and its matching map.

View from near Harts Point trail

Trail Name: H A T C H P O I N T

Map: *Canyon Country* OFF-ROAD VEHICLE TRAIL MAP - Canyon Rims & Needles Areas

Time: 2 hours; longer if any of the spur trails are explored

Type: Spur

Mileage: 12 miles round trip

Difficulty: easy, with the trail surface largely packed sediments and drift sand, loose drift sand, rocky rubble and slickrock.

Access: this trail is a spur from the Anticline Overlook Road.

Trail Summary: this trail provides access to Canyonlands Overlook, a magnificent viewpoint on the westernmost tip of Hatch Point.

Trail Description:

   The trail spurs west from the Anticline Overlook Road about 9-1/2 miles from where that road leaves the paved Needles Overlook Road, and about 1 mile north of the spur road to the Hatch Point Campground. After crossing a small meadow, the trail climbs into higher terrain, going in a southwesterly direction. In about 1-1/4 mile, the trail reaches a junction. The spur straight ahead is worth exploring if time permits, but the main trail goes right here. In another 3 miles the main trail turns left at another junction, then travels for another 1-3/4 miles through pinyon-juniper forest to Canyonlands Overlook. The spur that goes right from this junction drops into lower terrain to end on a canyon rim after about 2-1/4 miles.

   The view from Canyonlands Overlook is one of the most colorful, awe-inspiring, beautiful and breathtaking in all of canyon country. It rivals such better known viewpoints as the Needles and Anticline overlooks, Grandview Point and the Green River Overlook on the Island-in-the-Sky, and Dead Horse Point. Many miles of the most vividly colorful stretches of the Colorado River gorge fill the foreground, with the river almost 1900 feet lower than the viewpoint.

   Far below, at the base of the sheer cliffs and mighty talus slopes of Hatch Point, the Lockhart Basin trail can be seen wending its tortuous way through chromatic redrock desert. Beyond the river, Dead Horse Point and the Island-in-the-Sky fill the northern and western horizons, while the red and white spires of the Needles District of Canyonlands National Park appear to the southwest. The Abajo Mountains dominate the southern skyline, and to the southeast and northeast, the gigantic, curving cliffs of Hatch Point continue into the distance, with the soaring peaks of the La Sal Mountains piercing the eastern skyline.

   The trail to Canyonlands Overlook is not very inspiring, but the viewpoint itself makes the trip well worth taking and the spur trails noted add further interest.

Notes:

1. The trail to Canyonlands Overlook has been re-aligned since most maps of the area were published. The present alignment is shown on the commercial map, *Canyon Country's* **CANYON RIMS RECREATION AREA MAP.**

2. This ORV trail may be improved in the future so that standard highway vehicles can drive to the overlook.

Colorado River gorge, from Canyonlands Overlook

Trail Name: H U R R A H   P A S S

Map: *Canyon Country* OFF-ROAD VEHICLE TRAIL MAP - Canyon Rims & Needles Areas

Time: 1 hour; this allows time for viewing and a short hike at the pass summit

Type: Connecting

Mileage: 6 miles

Difficulty: easy, with the trail partly graded dirt, partly packed sediments, slickrock and rocky rubble.

Access: this trail connects the end of Cane Creek Road with Cane Creek Canyon, Chicken Corners and Jackson Hole trails.

Trail Summary: this trail ascends the colorful sloping strata of an anticline, crosses Hurrah Pass with its spectacular views, then descends the same strata toward the scenic Colorado River bluffs, making connections with three other trails.

Hurrah Pass summit, Anticline Overlook top-center

36

Trail Description:

The trail begins where Cane Creek Road ends at a creek ford. The trail may get occasional maintenance as a graded dirt road between the ford and the Hurrah Pass summit, but more often is not safely passable to highway-type vehicles much beyond the ford. About 1/2 mile beyond the ford the Cane Creek Canyon trail spurs left, while the Hurrah Pass trail swings to the right and starts climbing the rocky strata of the anticline that gave Anticline Overlook its name. The rim fencing and pavilion of this lofty Canyon Rims Recreation Area overlook can be seen high above the Hurrah Pass trail to the south. As the trail ascends the western slopes of Cane Creek Canyon it offers outstanding views down into that colorful gorge and the weird erosional forms that dominate its lower slopes in the Hurrah Pass vicinity.

Short walks out onto the elevated peninsulas that project out into the canyon from the trail provide still better glimpses of this unique area. At the summit of the grade there are excellent views in all directions, with Cane Creek Canyon and its varied beauty spread out on one side, and the spectacularly beautiful Colorado River gorge and its countless tributaries stretched out on the other side. Beyond the Hurrah Pass summit the trail descends the sloping anticline strata then twists down a rough alluvial slope toward the distant river bluffs. As the trail drops into a shallow, rock-walled gulch it forks. For the purposes of this book the Hurrah Pass trail ends at this junction, with the right fork becoming the Jackson Hole trail and the trail straight ahead becoming the Chicken Corners trail.

Notes:

1. The trail junction that marks the end of the Hurrah Pass trail is not very conspicuous. It is about 2-3/4 miles beyond the pass summit, and about 1/2 mile before the river-bluff rim is first reached.

2. An "anticline" is a large upward bulge in the earth's crust the deforms sedimentary strata that would otherwise be relatively level. Both Cane Creek Canyon and the Colorado River gorge have cut deeply into the anticline herein described, with Hurrah Pass being very nearly directly above the summit of the bulge.

3. From the top of Hurrah Pass still better views can be had in both directions by walking out to the rims of the sloping terraces on each side of the summit ridge.

Trail Name: J A C K S O N   H O L E

Maps: *Canyon Country* OFF-ROAD VEHICLE TRAIL MAP - Canyon Rims & Needles Areas

Time: 4 hours; less if the trail around the rincon is not traveled all the way.

Type: Spur

Mileage: 12 miles round trip

Difficulty: moderate, with the trail surface largely packed sediments and wash sand, loose drift sand, slickrock and steep slopes of loose river-bottom rock and gravel which provides poor traction.

Access: this trail is a major spur from the ends of the Hurrah Pass and Chicken Corners trails.

Trail Summary: this trail approaches and circumnavigates a gigantic, abandoned meander of the Colorado River, with an old mining area and weird, colorful rock formations along the way.

Potash mill, from Jackson Hole trail

Trail Description:

The trail begins where the Hurrah Pass trail becomes the Chicken Corners trail, about 2-3/4 miles beyond the summit of Hurrah Pass on the Colorado River side. The trail spurs right at this junction, then descends immediately into a small gorge, while the Chicken Corners trail continues straight ahead. There may be a fence and gate just a few feet from the trail junction on the Jackson Hole trail. Beyond this gate the trail follows the wash for some distance before climbing out onto higher ground. There the trail winds through highly eroded terrain studded with fascinating eroded rock forms. About 2 miles from the trail start it passes the site of some earlier mining activity then continues toward Jackson Hole.

As it nears this spectacular natural feature the trail is somewhat confused by old mineral search trails, but the main trail travels up a shallow sand-and-slickrock wash for some distance, then climbs out to wend a tortuous path through the great masses of ancient river-bottom deposits left by the Colorado when it abandoned this immense ring-shaped meander. The trail completely encircles the high column of rock in the center of this "rincon," but may be easier to find going in the counterclockwise direction.

Notes:

1. Because of severe and continuing erosion of the ancient river deposits that surround the Jackson Hole rincon, it is not always possible to travel completely around the loop.

2. Rockhounds will find a wide variety of specimens in the river-rock deposits within Jackson Hole.

3. "Rincon" is a Spanish word meaning "corner" or "nook." It is commonly applied to loop-shaped canyons left when an entrenched river or stream abandons one of its meanders. There are many such rincons in canyon country, but only a few on the principal river gorges.

Trail Name: L O C K H A R T   B A S I N

Map: *Canyon Country* OFF-ROAD VEHICLE TRAIL MAP - Canyon Rims & Needles Areas

Time: 8 hours; longer if the spur trail down Lockhart Canyon is explored

Type: Connecting

Mileage: 40 miles

Difficulty: mostly easy, with the trail surface largely packed sediments or sand, with some rubble, slickrock and wash sand. The first mile of the trail at its northern end varies from moderate to difficult, depending on its current condition from erosion.

Access: this trail connects Utah 211 near the Needles District of Canyonlands National Park, with the Chicken Corners and Hurrah Pass trails and Cane Creek Road near Moab.

Trail Summary: this trail travels the broad, redrock desert benchlands that lie between the sheer walls of Hatch Point and the deep Colorado River gorge, between Anticline Overlook and upper Indian Creek Canyon, with outstanding scenic beauty all the way in all directions.

Colorado River, from end of Lockhart Canyon spur trail

Trail Description:

The trail can be traveled in either direction but is described here from north to south. (See Note #1.) The Lockhart Basin trail forks left up a shallow wash about 5 miles from the junction of the Hurrah Pass, Jackson Hole and Chicken Corners trails, or about 7-1/2 miles from the summit of Hurrah Pass. Within a few yards, as the trail is crossing an expanse of slickrock in the wash bottom, the remnants of an old rock wall can be seen beside the wash. This wall was allegedly built by stock thieves who held stolen animals in the spring-watered canyon for later recovery and sale. For the next mile the trail ascends this narrow, steep canyon.

Any appreciable amount of water run-off down this rocky but picturesque gorge can make this stretch of trail difficult, or even impassable. For the next several miles after the trail has left the gorge it travels the colorful redrock desert terraces that lie between the deep Colorado River gorge and the looming cliffs and great talus slopes of Hatch Point, providing continuous panoramic views to the north and west across the sprawling, wildly eroded terrain that lies between Hatch Point, Dead Horse Point and the Island-in-the-Sky. About 5-1/4 miles from the trail start it reaches a "Great Divide" where the trail crosses a ridge below jutting Canyonlands Overlook, the westernmost tip of Hatch Point.

From the Great Divide the beauty of the panoramic view is doubled because it offers views toward the south of the Needles District of Canyonlands National Park and the Abajo Mountains beyond, as well as the vistas to the north and west. The half-circle panorama from the Great Divide is outstanding, especially with the other half of the circle dominated by the soaring walls of Canyonlands Overlook.

Beyond the Great Divide the trail drops gradually and the view to the north is lost. For the next 16 miles the trail follows a circuitous path along the base of the Hatch Point cliffs, traveling around the deeper stretches of countless radiating canyon branches.

This part of the trail is outstanding for its variations in color and form of the eroded sandstone formations that are exposed on both sides of the trail. Rock hues vary from dark reds, purples and grays, to orange, yellow, white, amber and pink, with infinite shadings of these colors. The erosion forms are also endless, with tall, convoluted towers, gigantic stone mushrooms, rounded domes, undulating ridges and myriad shapes that defy description.

About 16 miles from the Great Divide the trail passes the site where the battered tail assembly of a crashed U.S. Air Force airplane once stood beside the trail, bearing mute testimony to the wild ruggedness of this remote corner of canyon country. In another 2-1/2 miles, as the trail crosses the lower, more open desert terrain of Lockhart Basin, a trail spur to the right goes down beautiful Lockhart Canyon. This trail provides one of the very few places in the region where vehicles can descend into its older geologic strata, in this case the Elephant Canyon Formation. This spur trail travels almost 6 miles down this twisting, picturesque canyon, past the scene of some earlier uranium mining activity, to end at the Colorado River. There is an old cabin near the trail end, and there are a few petroglyphs on the canyon walls near its mouth.

Beyond the Lockhart Canyon spur junction the main trail continues through red-desert terrain below Hatch Point, but much of the beauty of this stretch of trail has been marred by past mineral-search activities. At one point the trail goes beneath lofty Needles Overlook, the tip of another westward jutting peninsula of immense Hatch Point.

About 13 miles beyond the Lockhart Canyon junction the trail reaches picturesque Indian Creek Canyon. This stream ford is normally safe and easy but can become hazardous during or following heavy rain in the large area drained by Indian Creek. There are Indian cliff-dwelling ruins in the canyon walls near the ford. The trail ends about 3-1/4 miles beyond Indian Creek by connecting with Utah 211, about 3 miles west of the Indian Creek bridge and about 4-1/2 miles east of the side road to the commercial resort near the park boundary.

Notes:

1. It is recommended that this trail be taken from north to south, to avoid a long return trip in case the difficult canyon stretch at the north end is impassable. It is suggested that before this trail is attempted, advance knowledge of its passability at Indian Creek and the difficult canyon be obtained from local BLM or Park Service offices.

2. It was unfortunate that the beautiful and unique terrain through which this trail travels was not included in Canyonlands National Park, and thus protected from destruction by mineral-search activities.

3. This trail appears on the U.S.G.S. topographic map of Canyonlands National Park and vicinity, although the Lockhart Canyon spur does not.

4. In 1859, members of the Macomb Expedition explored down lower Indian Creek Canyon, seeking a way to the confluence of the Green and Colorado rivers. They failed to reach the confluence, but did reach the rim of the Colorado river gorge near the mouth of Indian Creek Canyon, and expedition sketches made of that picturesque canyon depict Indian ruins that can still be seen by hiking the canyon. The Macomb Expedition named this colorful canyon "Labyrinth Canyon," but the name did not become official. Ten years later, Major John Wesley Powell gave the name "Labyrinth Canyon" to a stretch of the Green River gorge. The full story of the Macomb expedition is related in the book, **CANYONLANDS NATIONAL PARK** - *Early History and First Descriptions.*

Trail Name: M O A B R I M

Map: *Canyon Country* OFF-ROAD VEHICLE TRAIL MAP - Canyon Rims & Needles Areas

Time: 6 hours; longer if the two spur trails are taken or if much time is spent hiking along the rim overlooks or investigating the archeological sites

Type: Spur

Mileage: 12 miles round trip

Difficulty: difficult, with the trail surface about equal parts slickrock, drift and wash sand, and loose rock.

Access: this trail is a spur from Cane Creek Road.

Trail Summary: this short but challenging trail climbs steeply into the sandstone fantasyland called "Behind the Rocks," offering views of arches, archeological sites, the Colorado River gorge and Moab Valley at various points along the way.

Colorado River gorge, from Moab Rim trail

Trail Description:

The trail leaves Cane Creek Road about 1 mile downriver from The Portal, where the Colorado River leaves Moab Valley, and just a few yards beyond a cattleguard in the road. The trail turns sharply left to climb the tilted rock strata that ascend toward the lofty rimlands that wall Moab Valley on the southwest. The trail almost immediately begins to ascend a series of steep, broken ledges. Between ledges the trail climbs steep slickrock, winding among large boulders and hardy juniper trees. Along this first challenging mile of trail the view back down the rivergorge is magnificent. Massive Little Arch can be seen in the cliff rim on the far side of the river.

As the trail tops out of this steep grade it turns right to closely parallel the Moab Rim, where a short walk to the rim almost anywhere will provide a spectacular view of Moab Valley directly below, the highlands of Arches National Park to the north and the Sand Flats and La Sal Mountains to the east and southeast, with the 12-mile length of the Moab Rim stretching off in one direction and the still higher ridges of Poison Spider Mesa and Gold Bar Rim in the other.

Moab Rim trail ascends the steep terrace, right-center

The trail closely parallels the rim for about 1/2 mile, then turns right again to descend into wildly eroded Behind the Rocks terrain. For the next 3/4 mile the trail is sometimes obscure as it crosses large expanses of slickrock. In this area an arch appears high on a wall to the left, beyond a wide stretch of sloping slickrock.

About 1 mile beyond where it leaves the Moab Rim the trail reaches an indistinct junction in a small level area. This junction may be marked by a rock cairn. The spur to the right is the main trail. The left spur soon drops down into a sandy wash, then travels up that wash. This spur eventually rejoins the main trail, but is usually difficult if not impossible to travel in the up-canyon direction. The main trail goes through still more severely eroded sand-and-slickrock terrain, then reaches a shallow drywash. The potholes in this wash may have water in them. It is well worth the time to hike down this wash to where it plunges down into a river-gorge side canyon. Generally, a deep step and pool of water block access to the final drop, but a hike up onto the slickrock rim to the right of this wash affords beautiful views down into the Colorado River gorge and of the first steep stretch of the Moab Rim trail.

Beyond the drywash the vehicle trail climbs into sandflats country, then ascends steeply up onto a huge slickrock dome. The top of this dome provides good views in all directions. The trail next descends from the dome, crosses a relatively level stretch of sandflats, then drops toward another shallow drywash. As it nears this wash the trail forks.

The short spur that continues straight up a low ridge ends soon, but is worth taking to the point where it drops steeply into a shallow canyon. Beyond this point a foot trail goes to where the remnants of a prehistoric Indian structure can be seen on top of a small, pedestal-shaped plateau. A narrow crevice grants the only access to the top of this easily-defended vantage point. Beyond this ruin, on the right side of the elevated ridge that extends in back of the tiny plateau, there are hundreds of prehistoric petroglyphs, plus a few names and dates old enough to be considered historic.

Back at the trail junction, the main trail goes left to cross a shallow wash, then ascend a slope where unusually hard, thin slabs of rock produce a metallic sound as vehicle tires roll over them. At the head of this slope the trail skirts around a small slickrock amphitheater, then climbs steeply through broken terrain to end at a second rim viewpoint overlooking Moab Valley, about 2 miles along the rim from the first one.

Notes:

1. Avoid further defacement of the petroglyphs near this trail. All archeological sites on federal land are protected by law.

2. Navigation on this trail is tricky in many places, and the first mile of the trail is the most difficult anywhere within the Canyon Rims Area.

View from one end of Moab Rim trail

Prehistoric ruins, near one end of Moab Rim trail

Trail Name: PRITCHETT CANYON-BEHIND THE ROCKS

Map: *Canyon Country* OFF-ROAD VEHICLE TRAIL MAP - Canyon Rims & Needles Areas

Time: 8 hours; longer if some of the spur trails along the way are explored, or if time is spent hiking to the several natural spans near the trail; somewhat less time if the optional Cane Creek Canyon Rim trail is used

Type: Connecting

Mileage: 27 miles

Difficulty: difficult, if the Behind the Rocks trail segment is used; easy, to the Hunter Wash area if the optional Cane Creek Canyon Rim trail is used; moderate-to-difficult in Pritchett Canyon.

Access: this trail connects Cane Creek Road with U.S. 191 and the Cane Creek Canyon Rim trail.

Trail Summary: this trail offers an excellent look at rugged Behind the Rocks terrain, several large arches, wild and beautiful Pritchett Canyon and a wide variety of sandstone erosional forms.

Trail Description:

    This trail spurs right from the Cane Creek Canyon Rim trail about 1/2 mile from where that trail leaves U.S. 191 about 13 miles south of Moab. There may be a sign at the trail junction indicating "Pritchett Arch." (See Note #1.) Within the next 1-1/4 miles there are three trail junctions. The main trail goes right, then left, then right at these junctions. About 1-1/2 miles from the trail start, a trail spurs to the right. This spur climbs along the rim above Spanish Valley, passing one large arch and ending below another small but very picturesque arch. The small arch can be reached by a short but steep hike.

    The main trail continues left from the junction through sand-and-slickrock terrain, offering views of the huge sandstone fins that dominate the southern end of Behind the Rocks. About 6-1/2 miles from the trail start, the trail reaches a large outcropping of red sandstone. A short spur trail along the southern side of this long ridge connects with the Cane Creek Canyon Rim trail near the west end of the ridge.

    There are two arches in this long ridge of weathered slickrock. The one high on the southeast side of the ridge is called Balcony Arch, and the one on the north side is called Picture Frame Arch because of its rectangular opening. It is easy to climb into the big alcove behind this arch. There, the span's name becomes very appropriate as it frames the wild and colorful scene to the north.

    From Picture Frame Arch the trail heads generally north across open sandflats, then drops into a series of shallow washes. About 3-1/4 miles from the arch this trail briefly joins, then leaves, the Cane Creek Canyon Rim trail. There may be signs at these two junctions which are both in a small, open canyon and just a few yards apart. The trail next climbs out of the canyon around a small butte, then continues through very broken sand-and-slickrock terrain for another 5-1/2 miles before reaching another major trail junction. Here, a spur coming in from the left connects with the Cane Creek Canyon Rim trail a third and last time.

    The trail goes downhill here, then turns left in about 3/4 mile. The spur trail that continues on downhill reaches a drill site in another 1/4 mile. About 1/2 mile to the left and beyond this site, this spur ends at a ridge which offers a good view to the north where part of Pritchett Arch can be seen, as well as another smaller span nearby.

    About 1-3/4 miles beyond the spur junction the main trail reaches the shallow drywash of the upper Hunter Canyon drainage, and junctions with two more spur trails. There is a breathtaking "dry waterfall" with a small natural bridge on its brink and a big, spring-fed pool below, just a few yards down this wash. The spur trail to the left here crosses the wash then closely parallels the right rim of lower Hunter Canyon for about 3 miles to end within sight of big Hunter Arch high on the opposite canyon wall.

Beyond Hunter Wash the main trail continues generally up a branch of the wash, and in about 1/2 mile a spur trail goes left. This short spur ends at the base of a cliff. A hiking trail goes from there to beautiful Pritchett Arch. There are still other arches along this trail and near Pritchett Arch. From a rock terrace behind this span it is possible to see Window Arch and Ostrich Rock in upper Pritchett Canyon. Not far beyond the Pritchett Arch spur trail the main trail passes a tall "chimney rock" beside a still higher cliff on the left. In this same stretch of trail there is a "window" high in a rock wall on the right.

About 1 mile beyond the Pritchett Arch spur trail the main trail climbs steeply out of the wash it has been following, then descends steeply into upper Pritchett Canyon. About 1/4 mile down from this summit an inconspicuous trail spur to the left ends in about 1/4 mile but continues as a foot trail to Halls Bridge, a large and beautiful arch in a huge sandstone fin that can only be seen edgewise from the main Pritchett Canyon trail. The hike to the nearest view of this span is short but quite strenuous. Getting directly beneath the arch requires climbing experience.

The main trail continues on down Pritchett Canyon between Ostrich Rock and Window Arch. From this vicinity it is possible to see the upper arc of Pritchett Arch on the southern skyline. About 1-1/2 miles from the Halls Bridge spur trail another spur trail penetrates a side canyon to the right. A small but interesting natural bridge spans this drywash about a ten-minute walk up the wash. The span is difficult to spot from the vehicle trail. On up this canyon there is a natural window high in the lofty wall that divides the canyon.

The main trail continues on down beautiful Pritchett Canyon for 2-3/4 more miles before ending at Cane Creek Road where the pavement ends about 4-1/2 miles from U.S. 191 (Main Street) in Moab.

Pritchett Arch

Notes:

1. The Cane Creek Canyon Rim trail can be used as an alternate route between U.S. 191 and the upper Hunter Canyon drainage system without bypassing any of the major points of interest along the way. This optional route, with a short side trip to Picture Frame Arch, is recommended for those not interested in the arduous challenge of the southern 15 miles of the Pritchett Canyon-Behind the Rocks trail. See the Cane Creek Canyon Rim trail description for making connections on this optional route.

2. The Pritchett Canyon-Behind the Rocks trail can be traveled in either direction but is more difficult to travel and navigate from the Pritchett Canyon end.

3. Allow two full days, either camping out along the way or returning, for exploring this trail and its several vehicle spurs and hiking trails.

4. The two arches noted on the first trail spur described can also be seen from certain stretches of U.S. 191 in upper Spanish Valley.

5. "Behind the Rocks" can be defined as the region bounded by Moab-Spanish Valley, Cane Creek Canyon, the Colorado River gorge and Bridger Jack Mesa on the south. This region is about 50 square miles in size.

6. Warning: there are steep sand hills on the first stretches of this trail that are sometimes very difficult to travel when they are dry.

7. This trail crosses a few yards of private property at the lower end of Pritchett Canyon. It is BLM policy to maintain access across this property.

Tukuhnikivatz Arch

TRAIL SEGMENTS

NEEDLES AREA

TRAIL DESCRIPTIONS

Trail Name: B E E F   B A S I N

Map: *Canyon Country* OFF-ROAD VEHICLE TRAIL MAP - Canyon Rims & Needles Areas

Time: 6 hours; longer if the several spur trails are explored

Type: Connecting

Mileage: 30 miles

Difficulty: easy, with the trail surface largely graded dirt, packed sediments or drift sand and broken rock, with some slickrock, loose drift sand and wash sand and gravel.

Access: this trail connects the Bobbys Hole-Ruin Park trail with the Cottonwood Canyon and Big Pocket Overlook trails.

Trail Summary: this trail permits exploration of the geologically unique highlands that lie between the Abajo Mountains and the Needles District of Canyonlands National Park, with prehistoric ruins and spectacular vistas as highlights along the trail.

Trail Description:

For the purposes of this book the Beef Basin trail is defined as the continuation of the Cottonwood Canyon trail beyond the Big Pocket Overlook trail junction. From this three-trail junction near the base of looming Cathedral Butte the Beef Basin trail continues, skirting around upper Salt Creek Canyon with fascinating views down into this colorful labyrinth. In this area and for the next several miles the dense native pinyon-juniper forests have been "chained" in large areas. The trail climbs continuously, traveling the steep northern slopes of Boundary Butte and other Abajo highlands, then reaches a major trail junction. Here, the Elk Ridge Forest Service road heads left, or south, while the Beef Basin trail continues in a northward direction.

For the next 6 miles the panoramas visible from the trail are outstanding as the trail drops into the intermediate levels between the Abajos and the Needles District of Canyonlands National Park. Eventually the trail crosses a low ridge and drops into House Park, the first of several broad park-like meadow areas in this vicinity. About 1 mile beyond the ridge, and again 1/2 mile farther on, short spur trails to the left are worth exploring. The first goes to a small ruin in a cave. The second ends at a picturesque old log cabin.

About 1 mile beyond the log cabin spur junction the main trail reaches a major trail junction in a small, open valley. Here, the Bobbys Hole-Ruin Park trail goes right while the dead-end loop part of the Beef Basin trail continues on to climb a low ridge, then drop gradually down toward the broad, open meadows of Beef Basin. A big, looping trail circumnavigates this scenic basin, with several spur trails along the way that are worth exploring. This loop can be explored in either direction but is described here traveling counterclockwise.

At the loop trail junction in the eastern end of Beef Basin the route goes right. Within 1/4 mile a trail spurs left. This is a short loop that is worth exploring if time permits but the big loop route continues west.

After several miles the trail drops down to cross the upper wash of Gypsum Canyon. It is worth the time to hike down this wash to its first big drops. Beyond the wash the trail continues to skirt around the basin along its wooded south side. Just past Sweet Alice Canyon one short spur trail to the left goes to a ruin, while the next spur left is the other end of the short loop noted earlier. Just beyond the short loop junction another spur trail goes right up Ruin Canyon. There is a small ruin on a low hill near this junction, a small cliff dwelling about 1/2 mile up the canyon on the left, and another in a cliff opposite where this badly eroded trail finally becomes totally impassable, about 2-1/2 miles up the canyon.

Beyond the Ruin Canyon trail junction the main trail continues, passes a spur into lower Calf Canyon in about 1 mile, then in another 1/2 mile reaches another spur to the right that is well worth exploring. This spur enters and travels scenic Beef Basin Wash, a narrow, twisting, picturesque canyon that is delightful. About 3 miles from the main trail this spur climbs out of the narrow canyon into an open, rolling sand flats basin. The trail continues but a short spur to the right here offers access to one of the most beautiful and well preserved ruins in the area. This spur ends at the base of a steep, wooded bluff and the cliff-dwelling can be seen high up this sandstone cliff in an alcove. The climb up to this ruin is strenuous but worth the effort.

Back in Beef Basin the main loop trail completes the loop about 1/2 mile beyond the last spur trail. There are other spurs in the Beef Basin vicinity that are worth exploring but off-road vehicles should stay strictly on existing trails in this archeologically valuable area.

Notes:

1. This trail is listed as a "connecting" trail, even though part of it is a dead-end loop, because it provides a useful connection between several other trails.

2. Do not climb on, or in any way damage, the many prehistoric Anasazi Indian ruins found in the Beef Basin vicinity. These valuable cultural remnants are protected by federal law.

3. There are too many ruins near this trail and its spurs to list them all.

4. Climbing into the cliff-dwelling noted in upper Beef Basin Wash can be hazardous and is not recommended.

5. A BLM sign beside the Beef Basin trail requests visitors to camp only in "designated areas." There are several such locations in the woods along or near the southern stretch of the Big Basin loop that are used for camping.

6. "Chaining" is done by dragging a length of heavy anchor chain between two large bulldozers, thus uprooting and killing all trees and large bushes, and converting multiple-use public land into single-use, for the alleged benefit of the cattlemen who hold grazing leases on the land. Reputable range-management scientists question the effectiveness of chaining, and it certainly violates the principles of "multiple-use," but both federal and state land administration agencies still continue this destructive practice.

Prehistoric ruins, near Beef Basin

Trail Name: BIG POCKET OVERLOOK

Map: *Canyon Country* OFF-ROAD VEHICLE TRAIL MAP - Canyon Rims & Needles Areas

Time: 1 hour; 3 hours if the spur trail along the northeastern rim is explored

Type: Spur

Mileage: 5 miles round trip

Difficulty: easy, with the trail surface largely packed sediments and drift sand, with some broken rock and slickrock along the spur.

Access: this trail spurs from the junction of the Cottonwood Canyon and Beef Basin trails.

Trail Summary: this trail goes to the tip of the high peninsula that separates upper Salt Creek and Lavender canyons, with outstanding views into and beyond these colorful gorges from the peninsula rim.

View from Big Pocket Overlook

Trail Description:

The trail heads northwest from near the base of Cathedral Butte to travel the length of the high peninsula between upper Salt Creek and Lavender canyons. The main trail out to the peninsula tip closely parallels the western rim in several places, providing excellent views down into and beyond upper Salt Creek Canyon. The view from the tip of the peninsula is magnificent. Big Pocket, a major alcove of upper Salt Creek Canyon, lies directly below, while the intricate, convoluted red and white sandstone walls of maze-like Salt Creek Canyon extend into the distance. With binoculars, Indian ruins can be seen in Big Pocket. Kirks Cabin, a pioneer structure, can be sighted near Salt Creek, and several large arches are visible.

The return trip from the peninsula tip can be made by taking a spur trail that zigzags along the eastern rim. At several points the views from this trail down into upper Lavender Canyon are breathtaking.

Notes:

1. The Big Pocket Overlook peninsula is shown on the U.S.G.S. topographic map of Canyonlands National Park and vicinity but the trail out onto it is not.

2. Although the top of this peninsula is not in the park the park boundary begins at its rim.

Big Pocket, Big Pocket Overlook top-center, aerial

Trail Name: B O B B Y S   H O L E - R U I N   P A R K

Map: *Canyon Country* OFF-ROAD VEHICLE TRAIL MAP - Canyon Rims & Needles Areas

Time: 5 hours; longer if much time is spent exploring the various spur trails and ruins

Type: Connecting

Mileage: 15 miles

Difficulty: easy, except for one very steep stretch, with the trail surface largely packed sediments or drift sand, and some slickrock, rubble, loose drift sand and wash sand.

Access: this trail connects the Beef Basin trail with the Elephant Hill trail.

Trail Summary: this trail travels the open meadows of Middle Park and Ruin Park with their several archeological sites, then descends through a picturesque lower canyon called Bobbys Hole, to join the Elephant Hill trail near Chesler Park in The Needles.

Descending into Bobbys Hole

60

Trail Description:

The trail heads north from the Beef Basin trail in the south end of Middle Park. There may be a sign at this junction. Within the first 4 miles there are several short spur trails that go to ruins or primitive campsites. The trail then drops into Pappys Pasture, crosses this narrow meadow area, then reaches the top of the steep grade down into Bobbys Hole. There may be warning signs at the top of the steep grade cautioning drivers to check the trail condition ahead before starting down. This is good advice. At the bottom of this rough, steep grade, a short spur trail to the left is worth exploring if time permits.

From this spur junction the main trail goes down the length of the Bobbys Hole canyon system, crosses an open sandflats area and a major drywash, then ends by connecting with the Elephant Hill trail within Chesler Canyon, near the Joint Trail hiking trailhead into Chesler Park. The scenic beauty along the Bobbys Hole-Ruin Park trail between the base of the steep grade and Chesler Canyon is outstanding, in an area in which unusual scenic beauty is commonplace.

Notes:

1. This trail also appears on the U.S.G.S. topographic map of Canyonlands National Park and vicinity.

2. Because of the steep, rough and eroded nature of this trail between Pappys Pasture and Bobbys Hole, it is recommended that this stretch be traveled in the down direction only, and even then with the greatest caution.

3. Do not disturb the prehistoric Anasazi Indian structures found near this trail.

Trail Name: C O L O R A D O   R I V E R   O V E R L O O K

Map: *Canyon Country* OFF-ROAD VEHICLE TRAIL MAP - Canyon Rims & Needles Areas

Time: 2 hours

Type: Spur

Mileage: 14 miles round trip

Difficulty: easy, with the trail largely packed sand and sediments, broken rock and slickrock. The last 1-1/2 miles are very rough.

Access: this trail is a spur of the extension of Utah 211 in Canyonlands National Park.

Trail Summary: this trail goes to the spectacular Lower Jump of Salt Creek, then on to a high rim viewpoint overlooking the confluence of lower Salt Creek Canyon and the Colorado River gorge.

Lower Salt Creek Canyon, near end of Colorado River Overlook trail

Trail Description:

The trail heads north from the paved road that enters the Needles District of Canyonlands National Park via Utah 211, about 1 mile west of the spur road to the commercial resort, at a Park Service information station. For the first mile, the trail crosses open sandflats and drywashes. It then roughly parallels the open middle stretches of Salt Creek until it reaches the Lower Jump, where the watercourse drops abruptly over an undercut rim into an immense chasm. This drop marks the beginning of the great lower gorge of Salt Creek Canyon. The trail next crosses the wash above the Lower Jump and continues through broken, rocky country in a northward, then westward direction.

About 3-1/2 miles from the Lower Jump, the trail becomes very rough as it crosses an expanse of sandstone. The trail ends about 5 miles beyond the Lower Jump. A short walk beyond the trail end leads to a magnificent viewpoint overlooking the Colorado River gorge. The river is almost 1100 feet below the viewpoint.

Colorado River gorge, Colorado River Overlook trail

Notes:

1. This trail is shown on the U.S.G.S. topographic map of Canyonlands National Park and vicinity, and also appears on a small Park Service trail map of the Needles District that is available at the park entrance station and various visitor center.

2. Since most of this trail is in the park, keep vehicles strictly on the designated trail.

3. Do not attempt to ford Salt Creek above the Lower Jump if the creek is flooding.

4. This trail may in the future be improved for travel by standard highway vehicles.

Lower Jump, Salt Creek, Colorado River Overlook trail

Trail Name: COTTONWOOD CANYON

Map: *Canyon Country* OFF-ROAD VEHICLE TRAIL MAP - Canyon Rims & Needles Areas

Time: 1-1/2 hours; 2 hours if the spur trail to the ruins is taken

Type: Connecting

Mileage: 15 miles

Difficulty: easy, with the trail surface largely graded dirt studded with rock outcroppings and damaged by erosion.

Upper Cottonwood Canyon, from Cottonwood Canyon trail

Access: this trail connects Utah 211 with the Big Pocket Overlook and Beef Basin trails.

Trail Summary: this trail provides a highly scenic access route into the unique highlands that lie between the Abajo Mountains and the Needles District of Canyonlands National Park.

Trail Description:

The trail leaves Utah 211 at the Dugout Ranch turnoff about 8 miles northwest of Newspaper Rock State Historical Monument and about 14 miles southeast of the road into the commercial resort at the park boundary. It begins as a gravel road but just beyond the ranch area deteriorates to a rough graded dirt road. About 3-1/2 miles from Utah 211 the trail forks. The right fork is the Cottonwood Canyon trail. It immediately fords Cottonwood Creek, then climbs onto the higher ground on the west side of the colorful canyon. There it continues to climb for several miles along the base of Bridger Jack Mesa before angling westward onto still higher benchlands.

In this area there are a number of spur trails, a few of them worth exploring if time permits, and large areas of native forest that has been "chained," a "range management" operation that has severely damaged the natural beauty of this area. (See Note #6 under the Beef Basin trail description.) This trail ends near the base of looming Cathedral Butte, at a trail junction where the Big Pocket Overlook trail spurs right, and the Beef Basin trail continues on between Cathedral Butte and upper Salt Creek Canyon.

Notes:

1. One spur to this trail about 5 miles beyond the creek ford drops back down into the canyon bottom near an old ranch structure and offers a view of some crude cliff-dwellings in a nearby bluff. This site is marked on the Mt. Linnaeus U.S.G.S. 15-minute topographic map.

2. This trail is shown on various Utah state and regional maps as a graded dirt road, but the unmaintained, eroded condition of the "road" makes it extremely hazardous to standard highway vehicles.

3. Do not attempt to ford Cottonwood Creek if it is flooding.

4. This trail appears on the U.S.G.S. topographic map of Canyonlands National Park and vicinity.

Trail Name: DAVIS CANYON

Map: *Canyon Country* OFF-ROAD VEHICLE TRAIL MAP - Canyon Rims & Needles Areas

Time: 8 hours; longer if much time is spent exploring the various side canyons by vehicle or on foot

Type: Spur

Mileage: 20 miles round trip

Difficulty: easy, with the trail largely packed sediments and wash sand and rock, with some water and mud.

Access: this trail enters beautiful Davis Canyon and several of its tributary canyons, offering an intimate look at several natural arches and prehistoric cliff-dwellings.

Trail Summary: this trail enters beautiful Davis Canyon and several of its tributaries, offering an intimate look at several natural arches and prehistoric cliff-dwellings.

Trail Description:

The trail forks left from Utah 211 just west of the Indian Creek bridge, and about 7 miles west of the Dugout Ranch junction. There is a Park Service register and a gate at the trail start. For the first several miles the trail winds over dark red sediments, then drops into the lower wash of Davis Canyon. There may be mud or wet stretches in the wash, depending upon the season and recent precipitation. For the next several miles the washbottom trail offers excellent views of such nearby promontories as the two Six-shooter peaks, then it reach the first low sandstone walls of lower Davis Canyon.

As the trail continues up the canyon its colorful, eroded slickrock walls get higher and higher, and there are lovely sidecanyons on both sides. About 7-1/2 miles from the trail start at Utah 211 it reaches the boundary of Canyonlands National Park. Here a grove of trees near trickling springs offers an excellent primitive campsite and a spur trail enters a small but lovely canyon on the right. Not far up this side canyon an elevated alcove in one slickrock wall shelters a beautiful prehistoric granary built under a natural arch.

About 1/4 mile beyond the park boundary a major spur canyon to the left contains several arches. About 1-1/4 miles beyond the park boundary the main canyon forks again. The trail may not be passable beyond this fork but at times continues up each major branch of the canyon for some distance. Still another spur of the right canyon fork

Granary Arch, Davis Canyon tributary

69

contains a high ledge with several stone cliff-dwellings and one unique dwelling made of logs, while the trail in the main fork ends below a curious natural bridge in a ledge above the trail to the left. The left canyon fork also presents highlights in the form of arches and beautiful sandstone walls. Every tributary of Davis Canyon has unusual beauty to offer those who hike beyond the ends of the vehicle trail spurs.

Notes:

1. Most of this trail travels in the Davis Canyon washbottom. Thus heavy rains can close the trail for several days, from flooding and subsequent run-off. If heavy rains seem pending explorers are advised to leave Davis Canyon as quickly as practical.

2. Do not litter, bury or burn trash in this lovely, unspoiled canyon. Bring all refuse out for deposit in the Park Service containers at the trail start.

3. Part of the described trail appears on a small Park Service trail map of the Needles District that is available at the park entrance and various visitor centers, but this map is not accurate in detail.

4. There are too many arches and ruins in the Davis Canyon complex to list more than a few.

5. The prehistoric Indian ruins in Davis Canyon are protected by federal law, whether or not they are in the park.

6. The Park Service may close some of the primitive vehicle trails that once penetrated far up Davis Canyon and most of its longer tributaries. If trail-closure signs are encountered, park and hike to explore beyond them.

Trail Name: E L E P H A N T   H I L L

Map: *Canyon Country* OFF-ROAD VEHICLE TRAIL MAP - Canyon Rims & Needles Areas

Time: 8 hours minimum; up to 3 days or more if all the spurs are explored and the major hiking trails along the way are taken

Type: Spur

Mileage: optional; up to 40 miles round trip

Difficulty: moderate, except for one difficult stretch going over Elephant Hill, with the trail surface including graded dirt, steep, rough slickrock, packed and loose sediments and drift sand, loose wash sand and rock, deep dust and loose rubble, with many rock ledges along the way.

Access: this trail is a major spur from the paved campground road within the Needles District of Canyonlands National Park.

Trail Summary: this trail with its several spurs offers access to many unique and beautiful backcountry highlights in the Needles District of Canyonlands National Park, and also provides access to several outstanding hiking trails.

Trail Description:

The trail begins at the paved turn-off into one loop of the Squaw Flat Campground in the Needles District of Canyonlands National Park. At this junction the campground roads go left, while the Elephant Hill trail continues as a graded dirt road toward Elephant Hill. About 3 miles from the campground the graded stretch ends at the base of Elephant Hill where the most difficult part of the entire trail lies just ahead. Here the trail first climbs steeply up a slickrock slope, then angles still higher on rough, broken rubble. At the top of this grade the trail crosses a stretch of relatively flat mesa-top terrain, then plunges abruptly down a series of steep ledges and narrow switchbacks. It is necessary to back down one switchback leg.

About a mile beyond Elephant Hill the trail reaches a one-way, clockwise loop. Going left here, the trail continues through wild and beautiful slickrock terrain and about 2-1/2 miles from the first junction reaches another. Here the left spur enters the Devils Kitchen primitive campsite while the main trail goes right to enter the Devils Lane, one of the many "grabens," or long, rock-walled valleys, in this area. It is possible to go either direction at this junction but the trail spur to the left will be described first. This spur continues up Devils Lane and in about 1 mile climbs through an offset in the narrow valley called "SOB Hill," for reasons that soon become apparent, especially on the return trip.

View of The Needles, from summit of Elephant Hill

About 1 mile beyond SOB Hill, the trail leaves Devils Lane and goes up the lower wash of Chesler Canyon. About 1-3/4 miles beyond SOB Hill the Bobbys Hole-Ruin Park trail comes in from the right. If time permits, the trip up this trail to the head of Bobbys Hole canyon is well worth taking, but it is not advisable to attempt the steep grade that ascends into Pappys Pasture, Ruin Park and Beef Basin unless the grade is in good condition. About 1 mile beyond the Bobbys Hole-Ruin Park trail junction, the main trail up Chesler Canyon reaches the head of the Joint Trail, a unique hiking route into beautiful Chesler Park.

The vehicle trail continues beyond this hiking trailhead for about 2 more miles up picturesque Chesler Canyon before ending. Back to the Devils Lane junction the trail to the right continues along this valley and reaches another trail fork in about 1-1/2 miles. Here the trail to the right is the return side of the one-way loop. The trail to the left climbs through broken, rocky terrain and in about 2-1/2 miles reaches another junction. The left spur travels down Cyclone Canyon, another "graben," to end in about 3-1/2 miles, 1 mile beyond a short spur that provides access to the Red Lake Canyon hiking trail. The right spur ends in 1/2 mile, within a 1/2-mile walk of the Confluence Overlook, a rivergorge viewpoint high above where the Green and Colorado rivers meet.

From either of these spurs, it is necessary to return to the one-way loop, then around it clockwise through a stretch of beautiful Elephant Canyon, and on back over Elephant Hill. Some drivers find the climb back over this rugged stretch of trail more challenging than traveling it the other direction.

Head of the Silver Stairs, Elephant Hill trail

Notes:

1. This trail is listed as a "spur," even though it connects with the Bobbys Hole-Ruin Park trail, because it is generally used as a spur. It is usually not practical to use the Elephant Hill trail for access into Ruin Park and Beef Basin because of the often one-way condition of the trail out of the upper end of Bobbys Hole.

2. The Elephant Hill trail complex appears on the U.S.G.S. topographic map of Canyonlands National Park and vicinity, and on a small Needles District trail map available at the park entrance and various visitor centers, although there have been some trail closures since the U.S.G.S. map was issued.

3. Most of the junctions along this trail are marked by signs.

4. Since all of this trail complex is in Canyonlands National Park, keep vehicles strictly on the designated trails. This Park Service regulation is enforced.

5. Heavy traffic and lack of maintenance combine to make this trail rougher and more difficult than it should be.

Trail Name: HORSE CANYON

Map: *Canyon Country* OFF-ROAD VEHICLE TRAIL MAP - Canyon Rims & Needles Areas

Time: 5 hours; longer if time is spent hiking to the larger arches and the Thirteen Faces archeological site

Type: Spur

Mileage: 15 miles round trip

Difficulty: easy, with the trail either packed or loose wash sand, depending upon moisture conditions in the canyon bottom.

Access: this trail is a major spur from the Salt Creek Canyon trail.

Trail Summary: this washbottom trail penetrates 7 miles up Horse Canyon, a long and beautiful tributary of Salt Creek Canyon, with several archeological sites and large arches along the way.

Paul Bunyans Potty, Horse Canyon tributary

Trail Description:

The trail spurs left from the Salt Creek Canyon trail about 4-1/2 miles from where that trail leaves the main paved road extension of Utah 211 in the Needles District of Canyonlands National Park, or about 3 miles from the spur that goes to Cave Spring. The Horse Canyon trail start is marked by a Park Service sign. About 3/4 mile from the trail start, a short spur goes left to afford a better view of Paul Bunyans Potty, a large cave-pothole type arch with Indian Ruins beneath it. There is a similar but much smaller arch in the same rock wall just downcanyon. This span is easy to spot on the return trip.

About 1/2 mile beyond the spur trail to Paul Bunyans Potty the trail forks. The left spur goes 3/4 mile to a view of beautiful Tower Ruin, high in the cliff behind a sandstone tower. The right trail goes on up Horse Canyon. From this junction the trail travels between the soaring, colorful walls of the gorge in the sandy washbottom. About 3-3/4 miles from the last trail junction, the main trail forks again. The main trail goes to the left. The right spur ends 1/2 mile up a tributary canyon. From there it is a 1/4-mile hike in or near the wash to the Thirteen Faces archeological site, where nine complete, and four incomplete, pictograph faces appear on the right hand rock wall behind dense vegetation. The hiking trail beyond the faces goes to a view of Castle Arch.

Castle Arch, Horse Canyon

About 1/4 mile on up the main canyon from this spur trail, some cliffdwelling ruins can be seen to the right of the washbottom trail. About 1-1/4 miles from the Thirteen Faces spur trail, a short hike goes to another view of Castle Arch. The main trail ends in another 1/4 mile. Here Fortress Arch can be seen, and a foot trail leads to this huge span. Horse Canyon ends a short distance beyond where the vehicle trail ends.

Notes:

1. There are other ruins and arches in Horse Canyon. Some are fairly easy to spot on the return trip down the canyon.

2. This trail appears on a U.S.G.S. topographic map of Canyonlands National Park and vicinity, and on a small Needles District trail map available at the park entrance and various visitor centers.

3. The location of the Thirteen Faces pictograph panel is shown on the South Six Shooter Peak U.S.G.S. 7-1/2 minute quadrangle.

Fortress Arch, Horse Canyon

Gothic Arch, Horse Canyon

Thirteen Faces, Horse Canyon tributary

Trail Name: LAVENDER CANYON

Map: *Canyon Country* OFF-ROAD VEHICLE TRAIL MAP - Canyon Rims & Needles Areas

Time: 8 hours for a quick trip in and out; 2 days or longer if the canyon and its many highlights are to be explored in any depth

Type: Spur

Mileage: 26 miles round trip

Difficulty: easy, with most of the trail in or near the sandy washbottom, plus a ford of Indian Creek.

Access: this trail penetrates far up beautiful Lavender Canyon with its many sidecanyons, cliffdwelling ruins and large arches.

Trail Summary: this trail enters magnificent Lavender Canyon, with its many spectacular natural spans, a number of prehistoric ruins and endless tributary canyons to explore.

Dry Fork Double Arch, Dry Fork of Lavender Canyon

Trail Description:

The trail leaves Utah 211 about 3-1/4 miles northwest of the Cottonwood Canyon trail spur at Dugout Ranch, and about 3-1/2 miles southeast of the Utah 211 bridge over Indian Creek. The trail goes across a cattleguard then turns right past a Park Service register. It next angles left past an old corral, fords Indian Creek, crosses an overgrown area of sandy washbottom then drops into and travels up the Lavender Canyon drainage.

About 8 miles from the trail start a shallow canyon spurs off to the left. This is Dry Fork Canyon, one of three major tributary canyons of upper Lavender Canyon. The trail that goes up Dry Fork for more than a mile is worth exploring. Just a few yards into the shallow canyon there is a small but lovely arch in the rock on the right. About a mile into the canyon there is a rare double arch partly obscured by vegetation, on the right just a short walk from the washbottom trail. About 1/4 mile farther on there is a large arch-roofed cave in the left canyon wall that has a hole in its roof, making it an arch of sorts.

Back on the main trail, about 3/4 mile beyond the Dry Fork spur, an obscure loop spur to the right goes toward a short side canyon to reach an elevated alcove that contains several cliff-dwelling structures. About 3/4 mile on up the main canyon, just beyond this, Caterpillar Arch is visible on the western skyline beyond a large, elevated sandhill alcove within the meandering cliffline.

Caterpillar Arch, Lavender Canyon

Just beyond the next cliff projection on the right, which has a cliff-dwelling ruin high on its southwestern face, the main canyon splits into two major forks. The washbottom vehicle trail goes up the right fork for some distance but must be hiked on to its sheer-walled upper end. There are at least three arches up this fork. The main canyon trail goes left from this confluence and offers several more ruins and major arches before it, too, can go no farther up the densely overgrown, rock-strewn wash. The largest span up this fork is Cleft Arch, about 2-1/4 miles from the confluence, about 1/2 mile beyond another arch high in the rock peninsula that separates still another canyon fork, and in a similar fin of rock that marks a short sidecanyon on the right. A short spur trail enters this sidecanyon and provides convenient hiking access to Cleft Arch.

Cleft Arch, Lavender Canyon

Notes:

1. Most of this trail travels in the Lavender Canyon washbottom, thus heavy rains can close the trail for several days from flooding and subsequent run-off. If heavy rains seem pending, explorers are advised to leave Lavender Canyon as quickly as practical.

2. Do not attempt to cross the Indian Creek ford in either direction if it is flooding.

3. Do not litter, bury or burn trash in this magnificent, unspoiled canyon system. Bring all refuse out for deposit in the Park Service containers at the trail start.

4. Part of this trail appears on a small Park Service trail map of the Needles District that is available at the park entrance and various visitor centers but this map is not accurate in detail.

5. Cleft Arch gets its name from the great lengthwise split in the span that can be seen from within the opening.

6. It is possible to hike up to Cleft Arch from the short spur trail that enters the sidecanyon behind it, but not from the main canyon.

7. The prehistoric Indian ruins in Lavender Canyon are protected by federal law whether or not they are within the park.

8. The Park Service may close some of the primitive vehicle trails that once penetrated far up Davis Canyon and most of its longer tributaries. If trail-closure signs are encountered, park and hike to explore beyond them.

Hand Holt Arch,

Lavender Canyon

Trail Name: SALT CREEK CANYON

Map: *Canyon Country* OFF-ROAD VEHICLE TRAIL MAP - Canyon Rims & Needles Areas

Time: 8 hours; longer if much time is spent exploring the many sidecanyons on foot

Type: Spur

Mileage: 30 miles round trip

Difficulty: easy, with most of the trail in or near the sandy washbottom, plus several creek fordings if there is any water flowing.

Access: this trail is a major spur from the paved road extension of Utah 211 within the Needles District of Canyonlands National Park.

Trail Summary: this trail provides access into one of the longest, most beautiful canyon systems within the Needles District of Canyonlands National Park, with arches and archeological sites along the way and magnificent Angel Arch at the trail end.

Angel Arch from behind, Salt Creek Canyon tributary

Trail Description:

The trail leaves the paved extension of Utah 211 within the park about 2 miles beyond the commercial resort spur road, and about 1 mile beyond the Colorado River Overlook trail junction. After 3/4 mile of pavement, the trail turns left onto graded dirt at a junction. In another mile, the Salt Creek trail turns right, while the graded road continues to Cave Spring. For the next 3 miles, the trail crosses rolling sage flats, enters Salt Creek Canyon then reaches the Horse Canyon trail junction.

About 1 mile beyond this junction, the Peekaboo Spring primitive campground is between the trail and canyon walls. There are pictographs on the cliff wall above the spring. For the next several miles, the trail follows the twisting wash bottom of Salt Creek, between colorful, convoluted canyon walls, past many small and inconspicuous prehistoric Indian structures in cliff alcoves, and through verdant canyon-bottom trees and vegetation. There are numerous sidecanyons along this stretch of trail that can take days to explore on foot, some of them with several large tributaries of their own.

About 8-1/2 miles beyond Peekaboo Spring, there is another primitive campground. There are some petroglyphs high on the opposite canyon wall. Just beyond the campground, the trail forks. The trail to the left goes to Angel Arch, about 1 mile up a side canyon. The trail on up the main canyon ends in about 1-1/2 miles, but provides convenient hiking access to the many points of interest farther up the canyon. The trail to Angel Arch ends in a dry creekbottom within a short hike of a popular viewpoint below this incomparable span, near another huge rock formation called The Molar because of its tooth-like shape. From this area, it is possible to spot other natural spans high on the eroded cliffs opposite Angel Arch, and a primivite, unmarked hiking route continues on to and beyond this massive span.

Notes:

1. This trail appears on the U.S.G.S. topographic map of Canyonlands National Park and vicinity, and on a small Needles District trail map available at the park entrance and various visitor centers, although this trail has been closed about 1-1/2 miles beyond the Angel Arch junction since the U.S.G.S. map was issued.

2. Since all of this trail is within Canyonlands National Park, keep vehicles strictly on the designated trail in the wash bottom. This Park Service regulation is enforced.

3. Since most of this trail travels the Salt Creek Canyon wash bottom, heavy rains can close the trail for several days, from flooding and subsequent run-off. If heavy rain seems pending, explorers are advised to leave this canyon system as quickly as practical.

4. Warning: there are patches of quicksand in Salt Creek Canyon, generally where springs seep up into the sandy washbottom. To avoid these, stay on the designated, well-traveled trail.

5. There are designated primitive camping sites in Salt Creek Canyon in addition to the two noted.

Prehistoric ruins and pictographs, upper Salt Creek Canyon

SUGGESTED MULTI-SEGMENT ROUTES

Canyon Rims Area

NOTE: The general directions for these sample one-day routes are given starting and ending in Moab. For details, refer to the trail segment descriptions along the way. In addition to these suggested multi-segment routes there are five excellent single-segment trails in the Canyon Rims Area that require one day or longer to explore. These are Harts Point, Lockhart Basin, Moab Rim and Cane Creek Canyon.

Colorado River gorge, from near Moab Rim trail

Segments: AMASA BACK/HURRAH PASS

Suggested Route:

Drive downriver from Moab and U.S. 191 (Main Street) on Cane Creek Road. Turn onto the Amasa Back trail in lower Cane Creek Canyon. Explore all the spurs of this trail, then return to Cane Creek Road. Turn right and drive on to the summit of Hurrah Pass where the highlands of Amasa Back join the anticline ridge that Hurrah Pass crosses, then return to Moab by way of Cane Creek Road.

Segments: CANE CREEK CANYON RIM/PRITCHETT CANYON-BEHIND THE ROCKS

Suggested Route:

Drive south out of Moab on U. S. 191, then west on the Cane Creek Canyon Rim trail, taking the short side trip to Picture Frame Arch. Continue along the main trail to its end, then return to the last spur that connects with the Pritchett Canyon-Behind the Rocks trail. There, join and follow that trail down into the Hunter drainage, hike to Pritchett Arch then continue on down Pritchett Canyon to Cane Creek Road and upriver to Moab.

Notes:

1. This route takes a full day to travel. Allow plenty of time by starting early.

2. At times it may be necessary to do a little trail work in order to get down Pritchett Canyon.

3. Taking this route in one long day will not allow time for taking such side trips as the trail and hike to Halls Bridge.

4. This route bypasses the southern half of the Pritchett Canyon-Behind the Rocks trail.

Picture Frame Arch, Pritchett Canyon - Behind the Rocks trail

Segments: HURRAH PASS/CHICKEN CORNERS

Suggested Route:

Drive downriver from Moab and U.S. 191 (Main Street) on Cane Creek Road. From the Cane Creek ford continue over Hurrah Pass and on the Chicken Corners trail. Take the spur trail to the caves, stop at the natural bridge by the trail and go on to the end of the trail. Return by the same route.

Notes:

1. There should be time on this route to go a short distance on the Lockhart Basin trail to see the old rock wall just beyond the trail junction.

2. If time permits on the return trip, sample the first stretches of the Jackson Hole or Cane Creek Canyon trails.

Pyramid Butte and Colorado River gorge, Chicken Corners trail

Segments: HURRAH PASS/JACKSON HOLE

Suggested Route:

Drive downriver from Moab and U.S. 191 (Main Street) on Cane Creek Road. From the Cane Creek ford, continue on over Hurrah Pass and turn right onto the Jackson Hole trail. Take this trail to or around the mesa in the rincon, then return by the same route.

Notes:

1. If the trail is not taken around the rincon there should be time on the return trip to sample the first stretches of the Chicken Corners or Cane Creek Canyon trails.

Cane Creek Canyon, from Hurrah Pass summit

SUGGESTED MULTI-SEGMENT ROUTES

Needles Area

NOTE: The general directions for these sample one-day routes are given starting and ending at one of the developed campgrounds in or near the Needles District of Canyonlands National Park, although it is possible to take them from Moab by adding about three hours for the round trip from Moab. For details along the routes refer to the trail segment descriptions. In addition to these multi-segment routes there are five excellent single-segment trails in the Needles Area that require one day or longer to explore. These are Davis Canyon, Elephant Hill, Horse Canyon, Lavender Canyon and Salt Creek Canyon.

Chesler Park, beyond end of Elephant Hill trail

Segments: COTTONWOOD CANYON/BIG POCKET OVERLOOK/BEEF BASIN

Suggested Route:

Drive east on Utah 211 from the Needles District to the Cottonwood Canyon trail junction at Dugout Ranch. Drive up Cottonwood Canyon following the trail to the Big Pocket Overlook junction. Explore this trail, then continue west on the Beef Basin trail. Explore the loop in Beef Basin and as many spurs as time permits, then either return by the same route, bypassing the Big Pocket Overlook spur, or camp overnight in Beef Basin.

Notes:

1. The option of camping in Beef Basin rather than returning the same day allows adequate time for taking the Bobbys Hole-Ruin Park/Elephant Hill route the next day.

2. It is possible on the return trip to go south by way of the Elk Ridge road through the Abajo Mountains. This road connects with the spur road to Natural Bridges National Monument from Utah 95.

Big Pocket, upper Salt Creek Canyon, Big Pocket Overlook

Segments: BOBBYS HOLE-RUIN PARK/ELEPHANT HILL

Suggested Route:

Either drive to Ruin Park from the Needles District via Utah 211 and the Cottonwood Canyon and Beef Basin trails, or take the Bobbys Hole-Ruin Park trail from Beef Basin if the night was spent there as suggested in the previous route description. From Beef Basin take the Bobbys Hole-Ruin Park trail through Ruin Park, Pappys Pasture and down into Bobbys Hole. There, continue on to where the trail connects with the Elephant Hill trail in Chesler Canyon. If time permits take the Joint Trail hike, the Confluence Overlook or the Cyclone Canyon spurs, then go over Elephant Hill to the Needles District starting point.

Notes:

1. It is possible to take this route from either starting point but there will be more time to enjoy its outstanding beauty, and perhaps take one or more of the Elephant Hill spur trails along the way, from the Beef Basin starting point.

2. Due to the uncertain condition of the steep trail section that connects Bobbys Hole canyon with Ruin Park, it is not recommended that this route be taken in the opposite direction.

Prehistoric dwelling, Ruin Park

94

AUTHOR'S FAVORITE TRAILS

As an aid to canyon country visitors who have very limited time in which to explore this fascinating land, I have listed below my favorite trail segments in the Canyon Rims and Needles areas. I made the selection on the basis of scenic beauty and variety, with only minor consideration given to the challenge of the trail. The choice was not easy because every trail segment listed in this book has much to offer. In more than two decades of exploring southeastern Utah's backcountry I have traveled every one of these trails, some many times, and have never failed each trip to see some aspect of beauty that I had missed before. That's the way it is in canyon country - more beauty and variety than can possibly be seen, even in a lifetime.

Canyon Rims Area

Lockhart Basin
Pritchett Canyon-Behind the Rocks
Moab Rim
Cane Creek Canyon
Cane Creek Canyon Rim

Needles Area

Elephant Hill
Salt Creek Canyon
Lavender Canyon
Bobbys Hole-Ruin Park
Big Pocket Overlook

I hope this book adds to your enjoyment of canyon country exploring by off-road vehicle.

Fran Barnes

Upper Lavender Canyon, Cleft Arch in the distance

FURTHER READING

Those who wish to know more about the unique and fascinating canyon country of southeastern Utah will find other books and maps in the *Canyon Country* series both useful and informative. They are stocked by many visitor centers and retail outlets in the region.

The listed books are profusely illustrated with photographs, charts, graphs, maps and original artwork. The maps are also illustrated with representative photographs.

GENERAL INFORMATION

Canyon Country **HIGHWAY TOURING** by F. A. Barnes. A guide to the highways and roads in the region that can safely be traveled by highway vehicles, plus descriptions of all the national and state parks and monuments and other special areas in the region.

Canyon Country **EXPLORING** by F. A. Barnes. A brief history of early explorations, plus details concerning the administration of this vast area of public land and exploring the region today by land, air and water.

Canyon Country **CAMPING** by F. A. Barnes. A complete guide to all kinds of camping in the region, including highway pull-offs, developed public and commercial campgrounds, and backcountry camping from vehicles and backpacks.

Canyon Country **GEOLOGY** by F. A. Barnes. A summary of the unique geologic history of the region for the general reader, with a list of its unusual land-forms and a section on rock collecting.

Canyon Country **PREHISTORIC INDIANS** by Barnes & Pendleton. A detailed description of the region's two major prehistoric Indian cultures, with sections telling where to view their ruins, rock art and artifacts.

Canyon Country **PREHISTORIC ROCK ART** by F. A. Barnes. A comprehensive study of the mysterious prehistoric rock art found throughout the region, with a section listing places where it can be viewed.

Canyon Country **ARCHES & BRIDGES** by F. A. Barnes. A complete description of the unique natural arches, bridges and windows found throughout the region, with hundreds depicted.

UTAH CANYON COUNTRY by F. A. Barnes. An overview of the entire region's natural and human history, parks and monuments, and recreational opportunities, illustrated in full color.

CANYONLANDS NATIONAL PARK - *Early History & First Descriptions* by F. A. Barnes. A summary of the early history of this uniquely spectacular national park, including quotes from the journals of the first explorers to see and describe it.

Canyon Country's **CANYON RIMS RECREATION AREA** by F. A. and M. M. Barnes. A description of the natural and human history and outstanding scenic beauty in this immense area to the east of Canyonlands National Park, plus a summary of its outstanding recreational opportunities.